Mini MUSIC

BOOK 3

Songs written by:

____

(YOUR NAME HERE!)

Created By: Zachary Seckman
Catalog: KDP-MMB3-PC

ZSMUSIC PUBLISHING

music made just for you

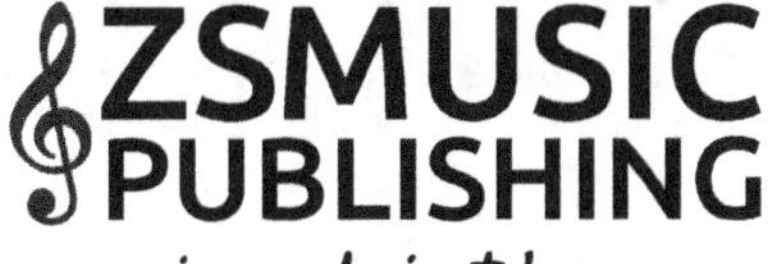

Through the MINI MUSIC books, students are introduced to various concepts through composition. In Book 3, students write 56 short songs through given sets of notes on the Bass Staff which leads up to learning 5-finger scales of C and G Major, and D Minor. This book is set up for students to write out notes in 4 measures using 4/4 and 3/4 times. The final two songs are blank 8 measure songs for students to write "longer" pieces.

There is also a good mix of titled and untitled songs. Most songs give students prompts to give them inspiration before writing, and some include a blank title for students to come up with their own. Creativity is the goal here, and students should enjoy the composing process. This book gives students a chance to do so, in small chunks so you can fit them in lessons!

In this part of the book, we will use the C-D-E notes. Write a song by adding one more Quarter Note in each measure below. When you're done try playing your song to see how it sounds! To finish, title your song!

TITLE: ___________________________________

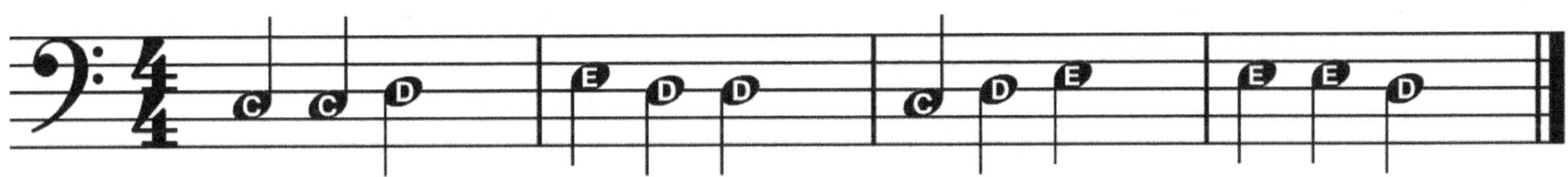

TITLE: <u>C-D Tracks</u>

Do you know what CD's are? Do your parents still listen to them? What would your "CD Track" sound like?

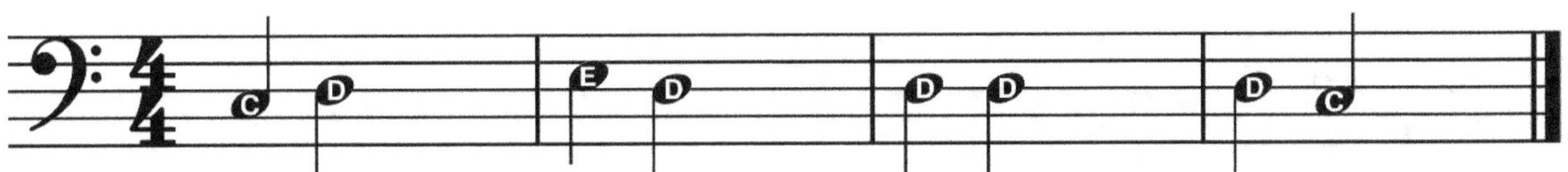

TITLE: <u>HIGHS AND LOWS</u>

Give each measure one more quarter note using the notes C-D-E.

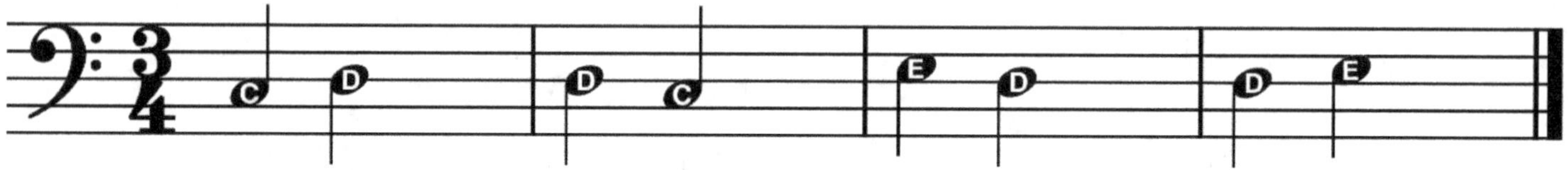

TITLE: <u>TEETER TOTTER</u>

Have you ever had fun riding in a Teeter-Totter with a friend? Using the C-D-E notes, give each measure three more quarter notes to make this song sound like you're riding the Teeter-Totter.

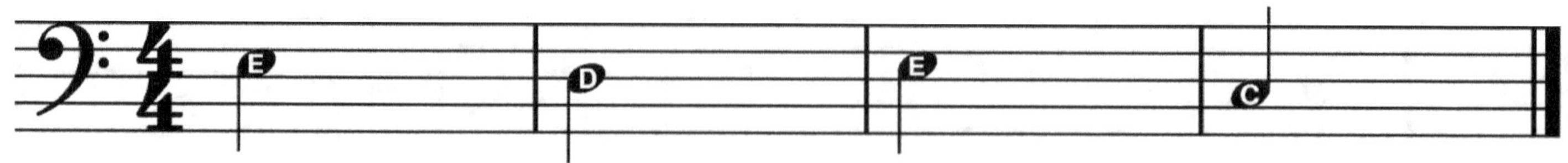

Have you ever seen a cat try to bat something with it's paw? Write this song to sound like a cat batting at it's toys using C-D-E. Fill in the blank measures below with four quarter notes, then title your song.

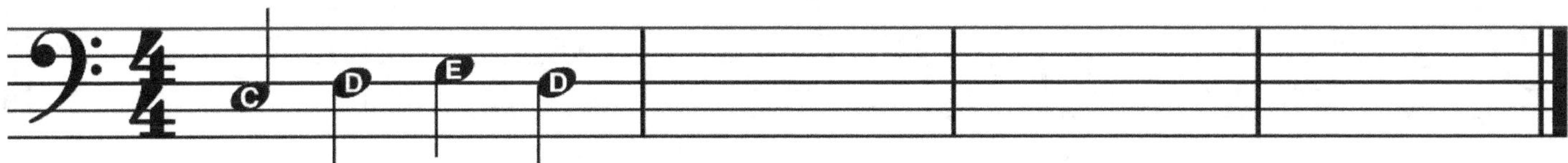

In this part of the book, we will use the C-D-E-F notes. Write a song by adding one more Quarter Note in each measure below. When you're done try playing your song to see how it sounds! To finish, title your song!

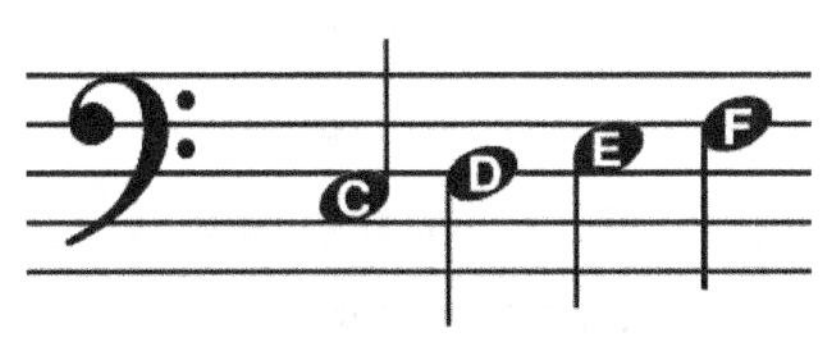

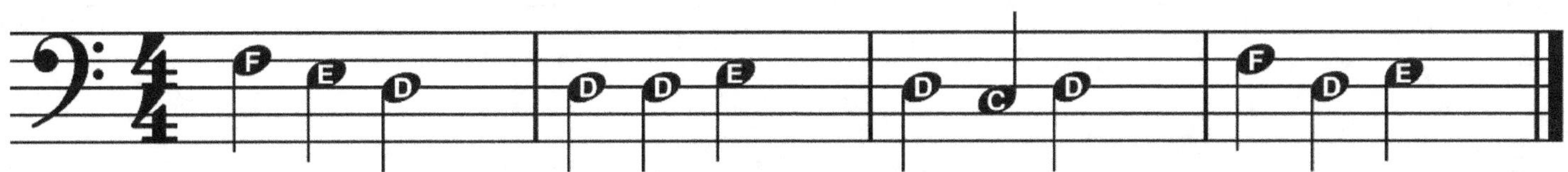

TITLE: _______________________________

Complete this song with the notes C-D-E-F by filling in the measure with two more quarter notes. Remember to give this song a title!

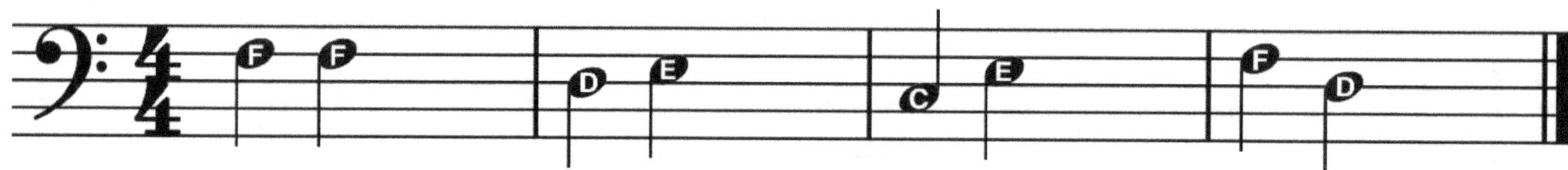

TITLE: <u>RUNNING ON UP</u>

Do you see what the notes are doing? They're moving up the staff! With the notes C-D-E-F, give each measure one more quarter note to finish the song!

TITLE: FLOATING DOWN

Think of what happens when a feather drops down. With the notes C-D-E-F, come up with a song that is like a falling feather. Each measure needs three more quarter notes.

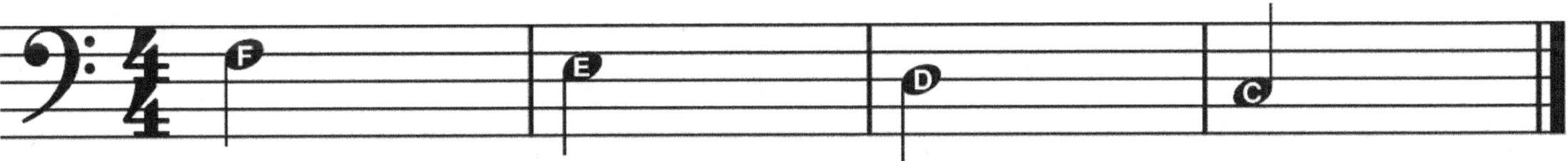

TITLE: THE TURTLE

If Rabbits are fast, Turtles are slow! Think of a "slow" song with the notes C-D-E-F and fill in the blank measures with 4 quarter notes.

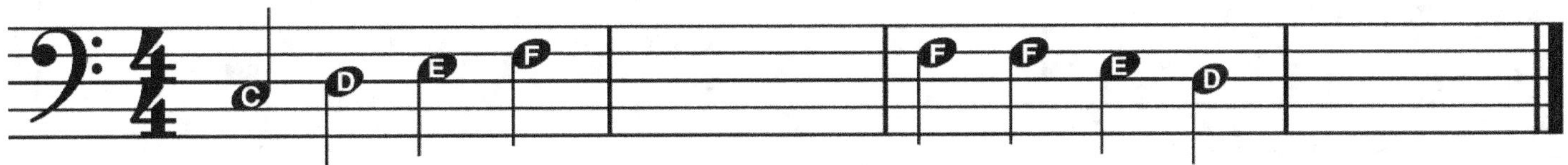

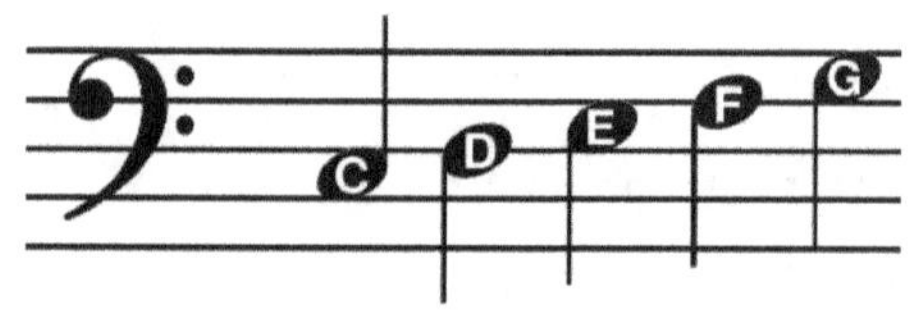

In this part of the book, we will use the C-D-E-F-G notes. Write a song by adding one more Quarter Note in each measure below. When you're done try playing your song to see how it sounds! To finish, title your song!

TITLE: ____

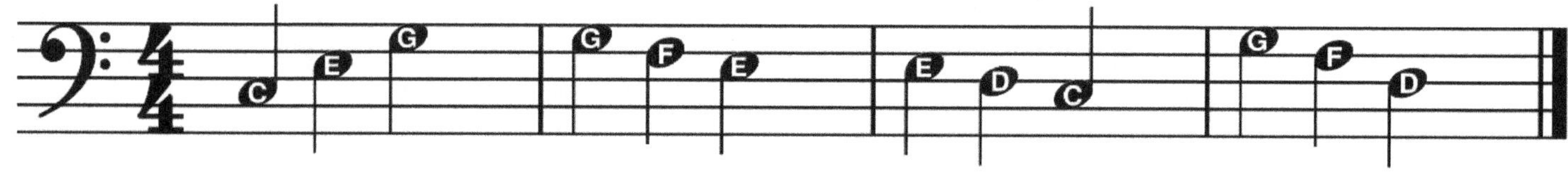

TITLE: <u>DOWNWARD</u>

Still using C-D-E-F-G, come up with a song that would make you think of hills, that gently go down. Fill in each measure with two more quarter notes.

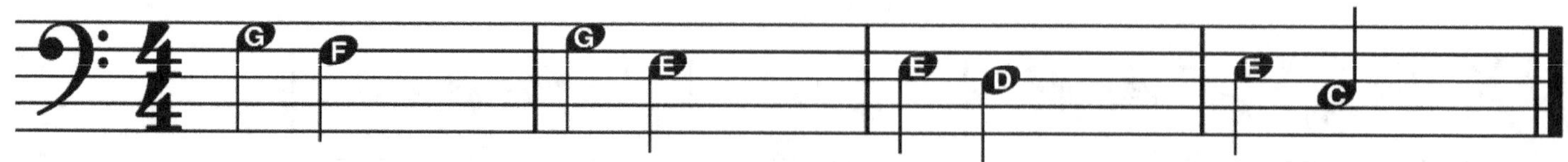

TITLE: <u>A SHORT RIDE</u>

Something that cures boredom is a short ride in a vehicle. Using the notes
C-D-E-F-G, fill in the measures with two more quarter notes!

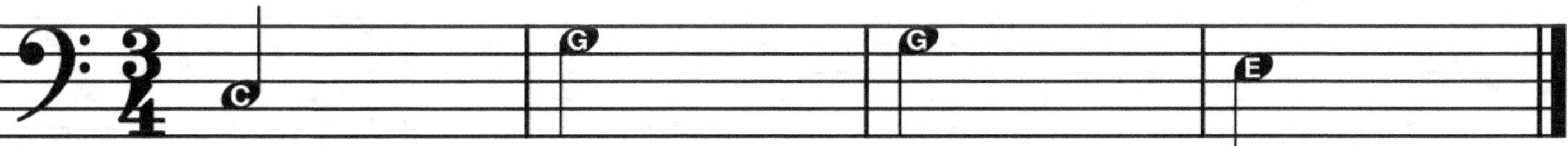

TITLE: ____

You're playing outside when you feel a gentle breeze in the air. How does this
make you feel? Use the notes C-D-E-F-G and fill in each measure with three
more quarter notes.

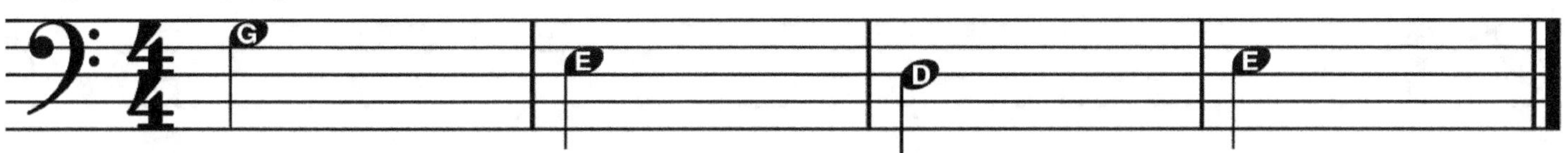

TITLE: ____

Write a fun song with C-D-E-F-G and title it! Remember that the empty measures
need to have four quarter notes in them!

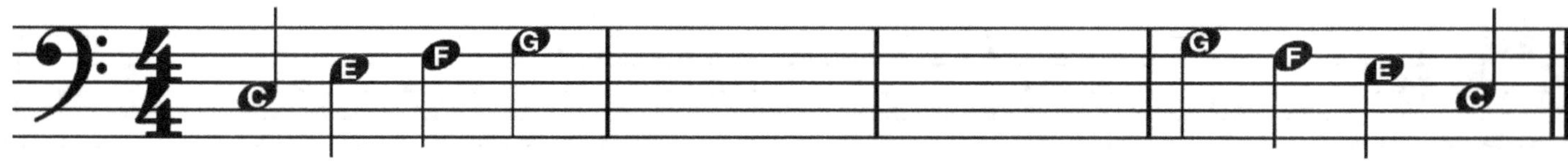

TITLE: <u>A COLD BEVERAGE</u>

It's so hot outside! You need to warm up with some Juice or Water. What feeling
do you get from the beverage? Using C-D-E-F-G, write a whole song on your own
thinking of that drink! Each measure needs four quarter notes.

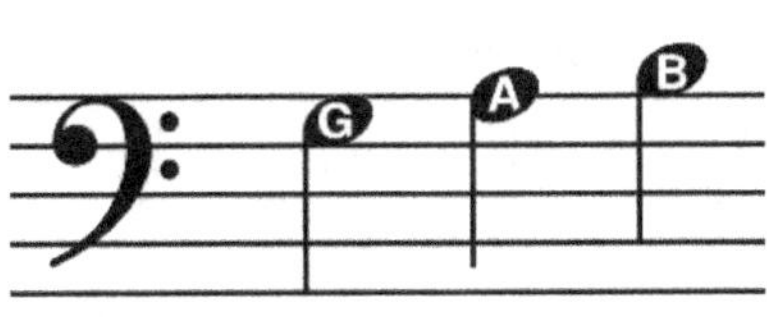

In this part of the book, we will use the G-A-B notes. Write a song by adding two more Quarter Notes in each measure below. When you're done try playing your song to see how it sounds! To finish, title your song!

TITLE: ____

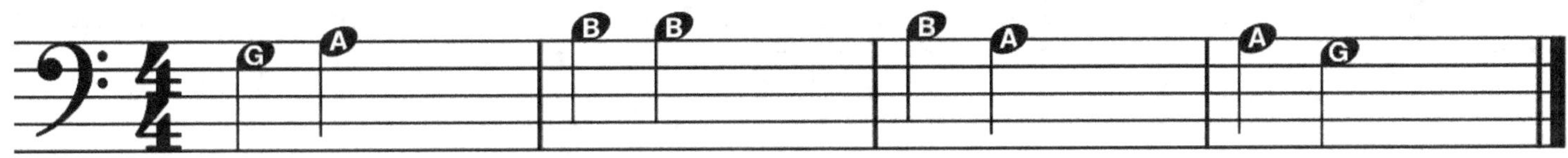

TITLE: <u>MY NEW BIKE</u>

Walking in the park isn't quite fast enough for you, so you want a bike to move about. Using the G-A-B notes, write a Scooter Song. You should add three more quarter notes to each measure to finish the song.

TITLE: ____

Finish out this G-A-B song with two more quarter notes in each measure, and then title your song!

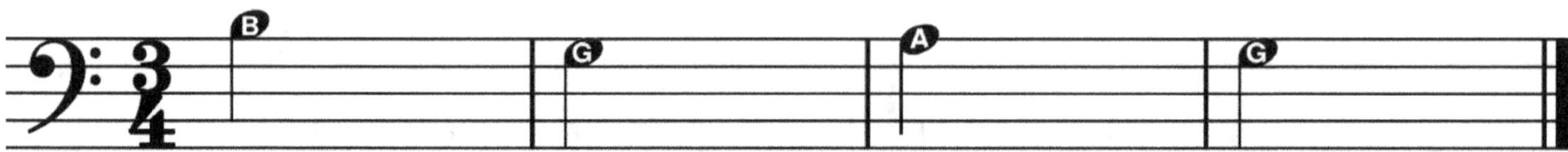

TITLE: <u>THE SPORTS TOURNAMENT</u>

The big game is coming up and you're excited for it! Write out this song thinking of the big game coming up by filling in the blank measures with four quarter notes of G-A-B.

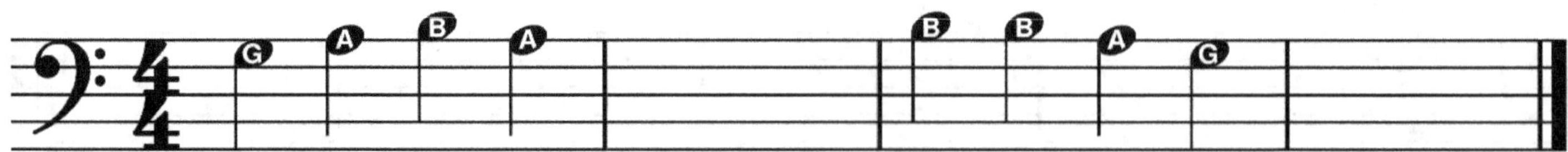

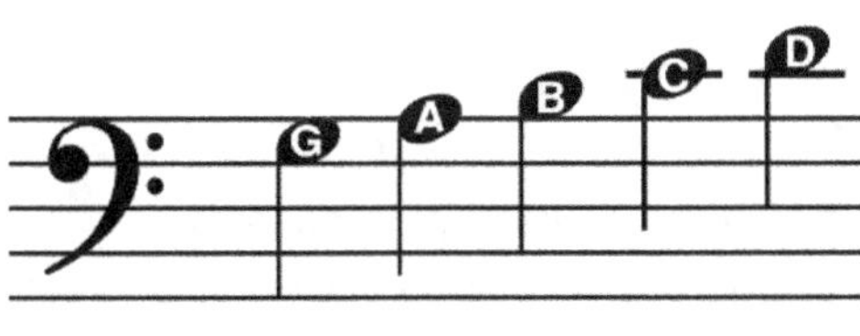

In this part of the book, we will use the G-A-B-C-D notes. Write a song by adding one more Quarter Note in each measure below. When you're done try playing your song to see how it sounds! To finish, title your song!

TITLE: ____

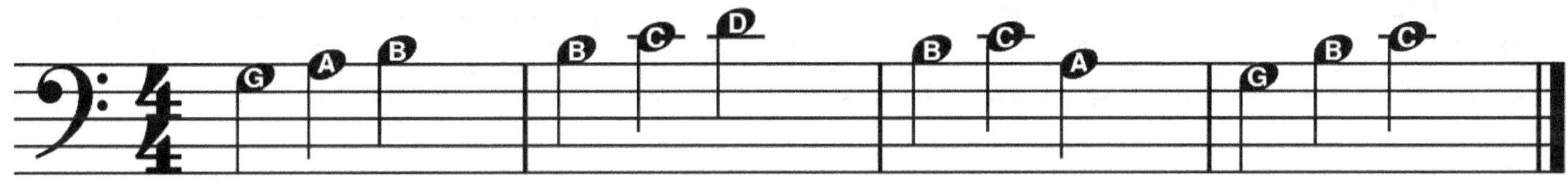

TITLE: <u>HIKING IN THE CANYONS</u>

Taking a hike through some canyons can be some hard, but fun work! Finish each measure to write your Hiking Song by drawing two more quarter notes to each measure using the notes G-A-B-C-D.

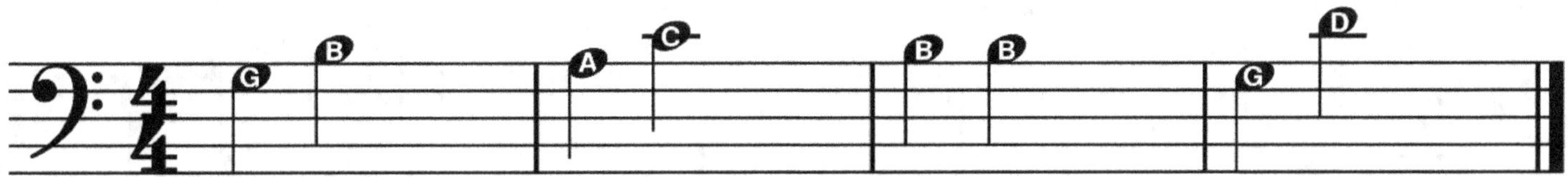

TITLE: <u>HEAVY RAINFALL</u>

You look up at the sky and see the clouds roll in and raindrops start pouring on you! How does this make you feel or think? Complete each measure by writing two more quarter notes in each measure using G-A-B-C-D notes.

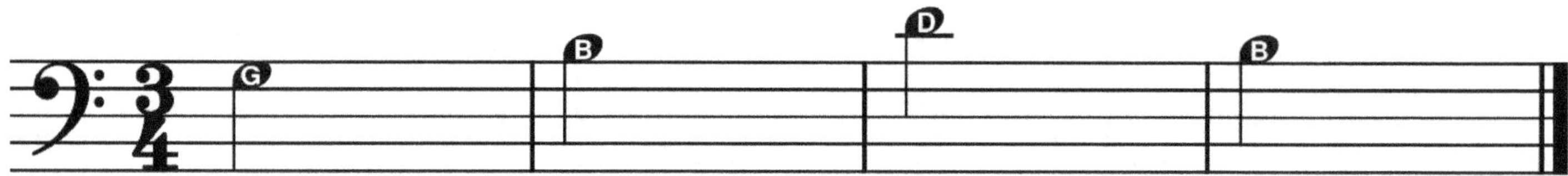

TITLE: <u>THE BOARD GAME</u>

You've planned a fun time with friends to play your favorite board game. Think of that as you fill in the two blank measures with four quarter notes using G-A-B-C-D.

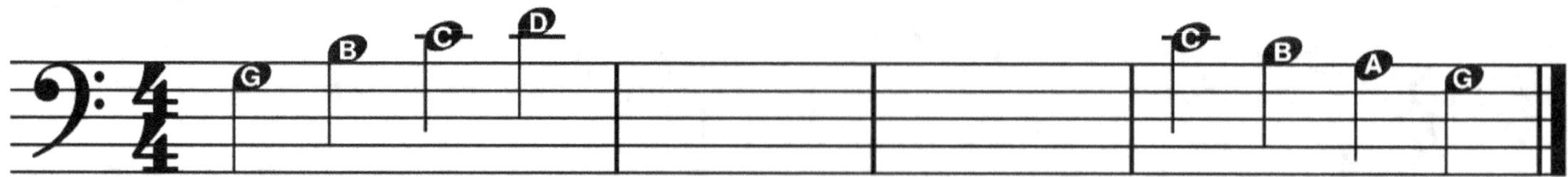

TITLE: ____

You're a late riser and today you woke up at 12 noon! Using the notes G-A-B-C-D write out a song about sleeping in late. Each measure should have four quarter notes in it. Once you are done writing, title the song!

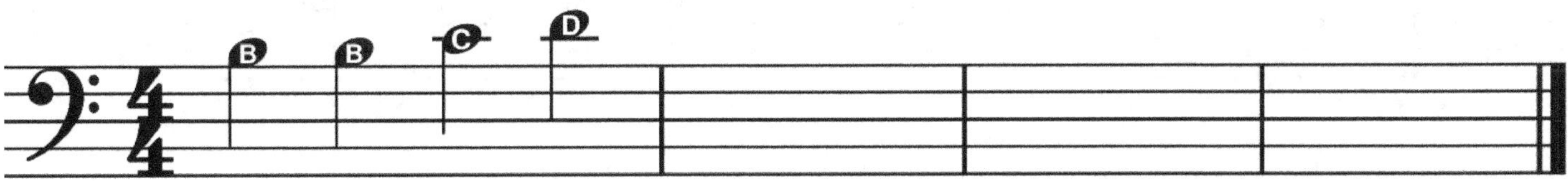

In this part of the book, we will use the D-E-F-G-A notes. Write a song by adding one more Quarter Note in each measure below. When you're done try playing your song to see how it sounds! To finish, title your song!

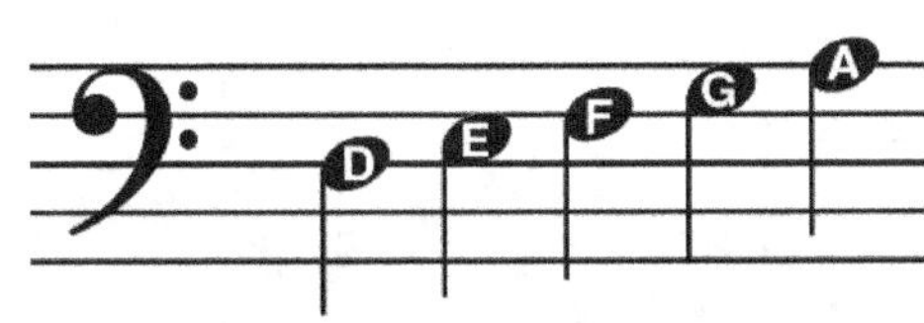

TITLE: ____

Come up with another song using the notes D-E-F-G-A, and give each measure two more quarter notes. Also, give your song a title!

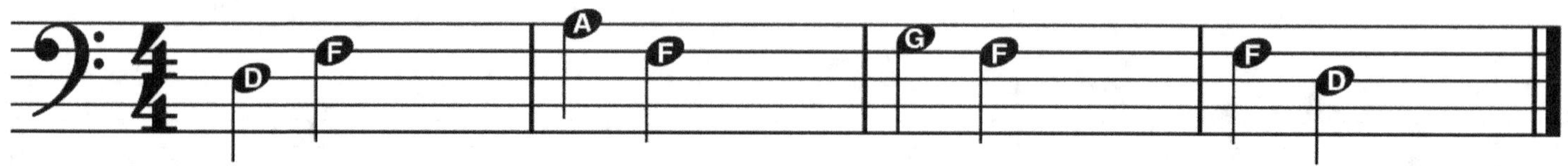

TITLE: <u>THE UNWANTED MEAL</u>

Ever have a meal that you weren't ready for but you were made to eat it anyway? Give each measure three more quarter notes using the notes D-E-F-G-A.

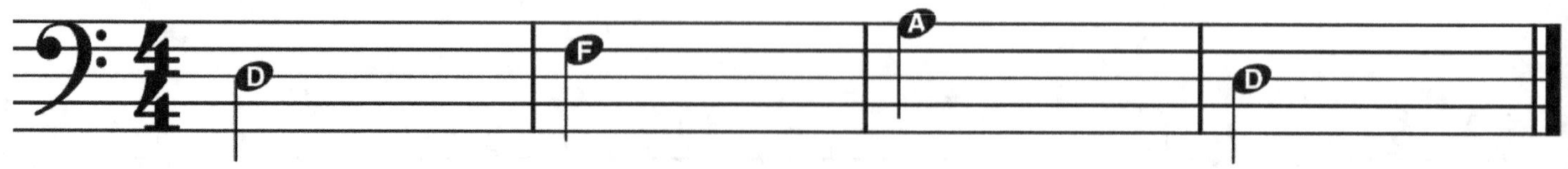

TITLE: ___________________________________

In this song, use the notes D-E-F-G-A and fill in the blank measures with four quarter notes. Once complete, give your song a title!

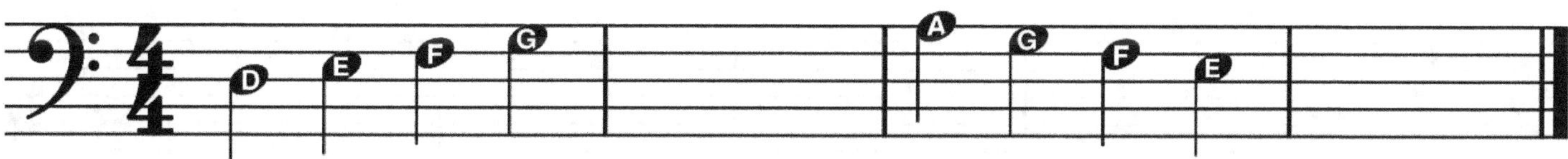

TITLE: <u>THE NIGHT LIGHT</u>

Sometimes, a light on when we sleep is comforting to keep the monsters away. Write a song with D-E-F-G-A about sounds that may frighten you at night. Remember that each measures needs four quarter notes!

TITLE: _______________________________

Think of a time when you couldn't wait to go somewhere, like a vacation!. Using the notes of C-D-E-F-G, come up with a "vacation" song. Each measure needs four quarter notes in it. Don't forget to title the song, too!

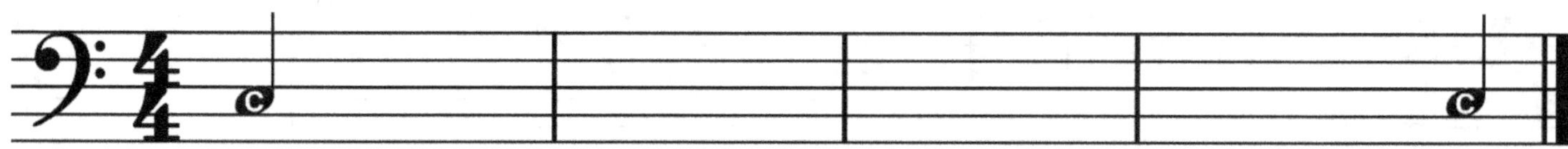

TITLE: <u>SECOND STRIKE</u>

Complete the song below by using the C-D-E-F-G notes. Each measure should have three quarter notes in it.

TITLE: <u>C TO MIDDLE C</u>

Using the notes of C-D-E-F-G, write out your song in the measures below. Each measure should have four quarter notes in it.

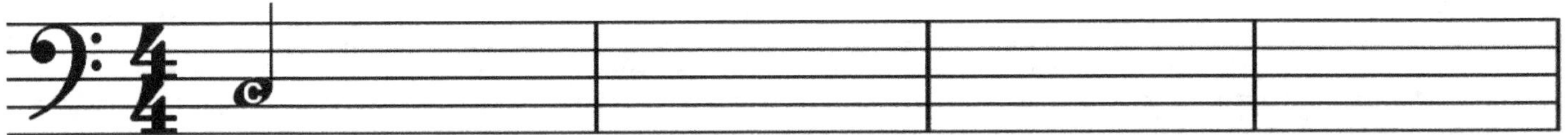

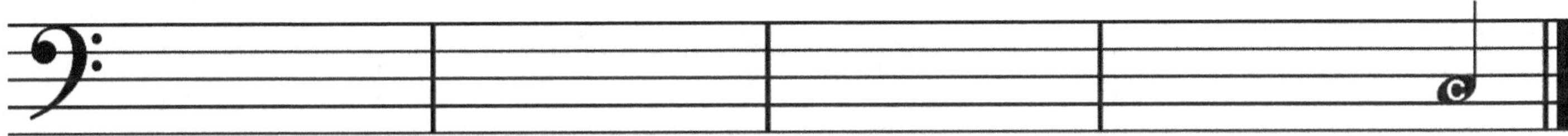

TITLE: <u>COMBO NUMBER FOUR</u>

Using any note you have learned in the song, fill each measure with three quarter notes to write your song.

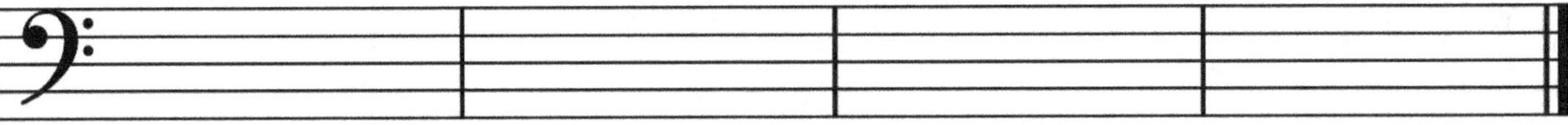

On this song, fill in the measures with any note you've learned in this book and title your song!

TITLE: ____

On this song, fill in the measures with any note you learned in this book and title your song!

TITLE: ____

On this song, fill in the measures with any note you've learned in this book and title your song!

TITLE: ____

On this song, fill in the measures with any note you learned in this book and title your song!

TITLE: ____

EXTRA PAGES FOR
MORE SONGS!

Hey Composer! The next few pages includes staffs that are blank so you can write more songs if you've already filled up this entire book!
Happy Composing!

On this song, fill in the measures with any note you've learned in this book and title your song!

TITLE: ____

On this song, fill in the measures with any note you learned in this book and title your song!

TITLE: ____

On this song, fill in the measures with any note you've learned in this book and title your song!

TITLE: ____

On this song, fill in the measures with any note you learned in this book and title your song!

TITLE: ____

On this song, fill in the measures with any note you've learned in this book and title your song!

TITLE: ____

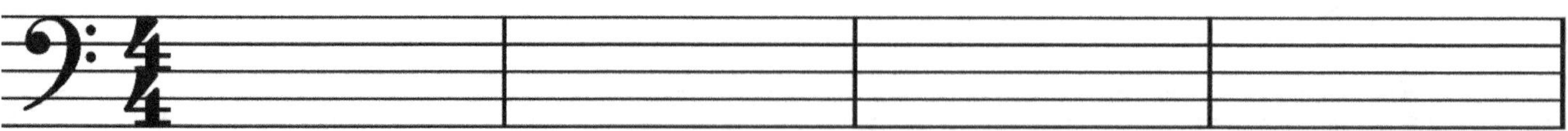

On this song, fill in the measures with any note you learned in this book and title your song!

TITLE: ____

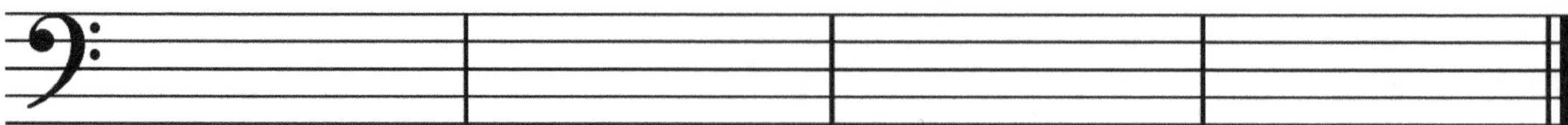

On this song, write in a time signature, fill in the measures with any note you've learned in this book and title your song!

TITLE: ____

On this song, write in a time signature,fill in the measures with any note you learned in this book and title your song!

TITLE: ____

On this song, fill in the measures with any note you've learned in this book and title your song!

TITLE: ____

On this song, fill in the measures with any note you learned in this book and title your song!

TITLE: ____

On this song, fill in the measures with any note you've learned in this book and title your song!

TITLE: ____

On this song, fill in the measures with any note you learned in this book and title your song!

TITLE: ____

On this song, fill in the measures with any note you've learned in this book and title your song!

TITLE: ____

On this song, fill in the measures with any note you learned in this book and title your song!

TITLE: ____

On this song, write in a time signature, fill in the measures with any note you've learned in this book and title your song!

TITLE: ____

On this song, write in a time signature, fill in the measures with any note you learned in this book and title your song!

TITLE: ____

On this song, write in a time signature, fill in the measures with any note you've learned in this book and title your song!

TITLE: ____

On this song, write in a time signature, fill in the measures with any note you learned in this book and title your song!

TITLE: ____